# WHEN RABBITS SPILL THEIR TEA

Metaphors to
Guide Us Through
Difficult Times

JENN BRANDEL, LICSW

*Jenn Brandel*

**MINDSTIR MEDIA**

Published by Mindstir Media, LLC
45 Lafayette Rd | Suite 181| North Hampton, NH 03862 | USA
1.800.767.0531 | www.mindstirmedia.com

Printed in the United States of America
ISBN-13: 978-1-7367342-3-0

*"A metaphor is something relatively more concrete or conceivable which stands for something more elusive."*
(Lakoff & Johnson, 1980)

*"A metaphor can be a conduit to material that has been buried alive."*
(Bayne and Thompson, 2000)

*"If a picture is worth a thousand words, a metaphor is worth a thousand pictures."*
(Daniel Pink, 2005)

# TABLE OF CONTENTS

# INTRODUCTION

ALL OF US HAVE A drive to find meaning in our lives, particularly during painful times. Without exception, each of us will experience difficulties, disappointments, struggles, and losses. Having a frame that helps us make sense of those experiences and find meaning in life's challenges can make those burdens easier to bear. Story-making and the use of metaphor can help us widen our perspective and stretch our capacities to cope with and hold our experiences, thereby helping us find greater meaning in our lives.

As a therapist, my clients' use of metaphor has been immensely helpful by evoking in me the empathy that allows me to better understand their stories. We learn from one another and join around the similarities we find among us. This helps us feel less alone. This is what communication, story-telling, art, and personal expression are all about. By using evocative words and images to describe something about ourselves, we allow others to relate to us experientially. Beyond having an analytical understanding of what we are saying, metaphors activate something deeper and more personal in us.

Metaphors allow us greater flexibility in our understanding and reactions and provide opportunities for us to shift our perspective and view a situation with some distance or from a different angle. They allow us to weave complex threads of our experiences into a single, simple, relatable image.

Metaphors allow us to identify and uncover meanings that may have eluded us initially. Reflection on a metaphor stimulates not just the thinking part of our brain, but the regions associated with touch, emotion regulation, bodily sensations, and motor activity. A metaphor can drive our power of thinking while also tapping our deeper body-mind connections. Some studies indicate our whole body may respond similarly to a real-life experience and a metaphorical description of that experience. This offers tremendous potential for healing.

# HOW TO USE THIS BOOK

*"Metaphors have a way of holding the most truth in the least space."*
(Orson Scott Card, *Alvin Journeyman*, 1995)

THIS BOOK PROVIDES EXAMPLES OF how metaphors may offer all of us an effective tool for reflecting on our experiences, finding what is relatable across differences and discovering new insights that may help us gain clarity, direction, and a sense of acceptance. It is meant to be experiential, to evoke in readers a very personal interpretation of every story and image. While it can be read sequentially, each page stands alone, allowing readers to flip through, browse and reread passages as they wish. Some readers may choose to meditate on one metaphor for an extended period, perhaps leaving the book propped open on a table or desk as a touchstone or reminder.

There are no right or wrong interpretations of the metaphors, they can be adapted or replaced with your own imagery. Your experience of each metaphor will be your own and what resonates will be personal to you. My hope is that every reader will find something in this book that is useful. An even greater hope is that what you find here will be shared with others who may be navigating their own challenges. Stories are one way of taking care of and comforting one another. May this small collection spark conversation, bridge divisions, and foster compassion in each one of us.

Note: While the development and commentary for each of these metaphors is my own, their formulation was no doubt influenced by innumerable sources, referenced when possible and sometimes less consciously attributed. Gratitude is especially given to the many clients with whom I have had the honor of working. Many of the images and metaphors in this book were co-created within the context of our work together over many years.

# THE METAPHORS

IMAGINE YOU ARE WALKING ACROSS a narrow balance beam. Your eyes are looking straight ahead and you are aware of every step, careful not to lose your footing. Now and then, you feel yourself slipping, your stomach lurches, and you instinctually reach out for something to grasp. Sometimes there is something there to help you steady yourself—the hand of a friend, a railing, or the comfort of a solid wall to lean against until you've regained your steadiness. Other times, there is only you and you must find ways to remain solid and grounded using only your body, your focus, and your inner reassurances to keep yourself rooted.

During times of struggle, we may feel terrified, unmoored, overwhelmed, lost, or off-balance. We may have the impulse to grasp for something external to help us cope. When these things are available and effective, we may feel reassured.

Our fear—and our willingness to take risks—changes when the beam we are crossing is a hundred feet up rather than one foot off the ground. More often than not, the risks we are facing are relatively manageable. Sometimes we need to feel the unsteadiness and even allow ourselves to fall in order to be reminded that we are okay, that failing now and again will not kill us. Having a realistic perspective of the risks we are facing may bolster our confidence, allow us to step more easily into change, and remind us of our inner capacity to recalibrate ourselves.

WHILE SOME OF US MAY feel a bit squeamish thinking about the process of childbirth, most of us have a general idea of how it goes. The most common scene that comes to mind is an exhausted person pushing and a baby slowly—inch by inch—making its way out and into the waiting arms of a doctor, nurse, or midwife.

Some of us may be surprised to learn that often the process is not as straightforward as we imagined. During birth, many babies move forward and backward as they exit the birth canal. They may start to emerge, then be drawn back in slightly, then come out a bit further—back and forth—ultimately moving themselves through the birth canal and out into the world.

At times, our own growth and transformation may be incremental. We may experience setbacks, relapses, or stumble on our path. We may feel ourselves making gains, only to be followed by a tough day during which we returned to old habits or ways of coping. Remember, it is all part of our process. As long as we continue to move forward, even with minor drawbacks, we will make our way through and ultimately emerge on the other side.

BOUNDARIES CAN BE MESSY. BEING mindful of what we are expressing outwardly and keeping our feelings from flying out of control and impacting other people is challenging. Even when we're working hard at being responsible for our own feelings, others around us may be less skillful—they may allow their emotions to spatter and overwhelm them and those around them.

Just like running a blender with the lid off, people sometimes fail to contain their fears, insecurities, resentments, and judgments. Their feelings may fly all over the place, covering us with a mess of emotional content for which we're not responsible. We may find ourselves hit by a slew of emotions over which we have little control.

Perhaps our boss who had a stressful morning snaps at us when we ask them a simple question or a friend who is feeling insecure questions the sincerity of our fondness for them. When other people's feelings pour out in front of us, it can be tempting to take things personally and to respond defensively. It can help to slow down, take a step back and be mindful of what directly relates to us and what may be emotional spillover from a different context.

Healthy boundaries allow us to share our feelings with others while taking responsibility for how our words and behaviors affect other people. They also help us identify the limits of our control and where another person's accountability lies. The next time you feel impacted by someone else's emotional state, check in with yourself. Does this feel like it is my responsibility? Do I have the power to impact or lessen this person's suffering? Or is this person simply having a feeling that is hard for them to contain? We can always respond from a place of compassion and empathy. Hopefully, though, we're able to walk away from the interaction without carrying an emotional mess that isn't ours to bear.

WE HAVE A RANGE OF options for communicating boundaries in our relationships, and we have the right to exercise those options as we need them.

Imagine you have a friend who is a hugger. One day, your friend enthusiastically approaches you, arms wide, to embrace you. You are feeling a need for space and would prefer not to hug in that moment. You start with a soft boundary—maybe taking a subtle step backward or changing your posture so your arms are crossed in front of you. If your friend is attuned and notices your communication, they may adjust and pull back, maybe shaking your hand in greeting instead.

If your friend misses the cue, or disregards it, you may need to express a harder boundary—maybe using humor and deflecting the hug, saying gently, "I'm not really in a hugging mood at the moment." Again, if the message is received and honored, this may be the end of it.

If your friend still does not receive the message and continues to approach, you may need to harden your boundary even further, possibly putting out your hand and saying, "Please stop. I'd prefer you not hug me."

If the friend's behavior becomes aggressive and persistent, you might need to go even further—perhaps seeking a legal means of holding your boundary, such as a restraining order.

Knowing our full range of options allows us to adjust our boundary to fit the situation. It probably isn't appropriate or in our best interest to start with our hardest boundary if a friend has demonstrated an ability to read and respect the limits we are setting. It may also be ineffective to continue to assert our softest boundary with someone who is clearly not paying attention or who repeatedly disregards our needs.

What are the ways you communicate a soft boundary? A hard boundary? What might you gain by making adjustments and giving yourself a wider range of options?

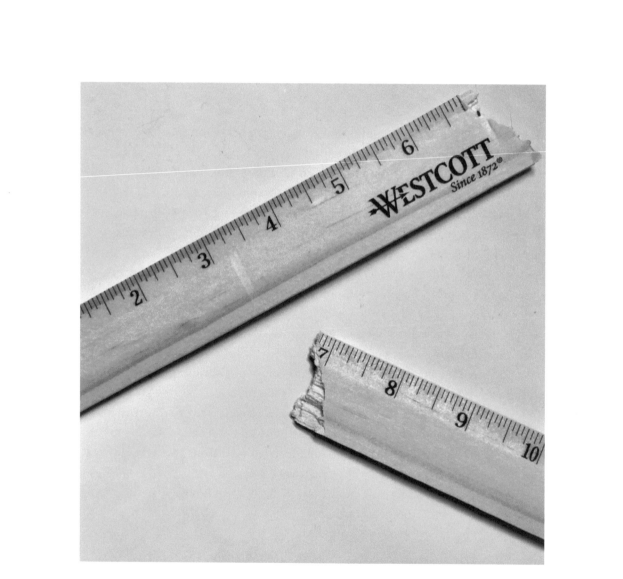

IMAGINE THAT YOU ARE HOLDING a ruler that has been broken off at one end. The ruler is old and worn, the markings impossible to make out. Now imagine that you are asked to measure a distance using only that ruler. You are told the outcome of your measurement is critical and will have significant consequences for the future. How much faith would you have in that ruler as a tool?

We are constantly sizing ourselves up, comparing ourselves to others, estimating our worth. We measure our value as students, not just by grades (which in and of themselves are often subjective and unreliable) but by how quickly we learn, how we process information, how confident we feel speaking about the material. We measure our value at work, not just by performance evaluations (which can be colored by other people's biases and may not reflect the whole of our contributions) but by how much money we make, how many hours we work, the job titles we have. We measure our value in relationships by how many partners we've had, how much sex we have, how attractive people find us. At times, we may find that the tool we are using to judge ourselves and our lives fails to accurately reflect our worth or contributions.

How might you judge your value if you found out the ruler you've been using all this time was flawed? To what sources of data might you find yourself opening up? Consider asking those around you what factors they consider when judging your worth and check their answers against your own sense of self. What might you learn by using a more flexible measuring tool?

IMAGINE YOU ARE LIKE A bus. Each rider represents a different facet of your personality and expression. There's the professional part of you, the sensitive part of you, the dependent part of you, the creative part of you. Some parts of ourselves are easier to accept and share with people than other parts. We may see the parts of us that are brave, confident, accomplished, or adventurous as more desirable and well-liked by people in our lives. We may show those sides of ourselves more readily and find those qualities valuable to us.

Other parts of ourselves we may wish to avoid. Some parts are loud, dramatic, difficult, or intrusive. The part of us that is fearful may keep us from taking risks necessary to achieve our goals. The part of us that is insecure may fill our thoughts with self-doubt. Sometimes we may wish we could pick and choose. Like a bus driver, we may wish we were able to close the door and keep some parts from getting on board. When parts of us get activated and start making a fuss, we may wish we could kick them out, leave them by the side of the road, or lock them away somewhere.

It is important to remember that all parts of ourselves—all of our qualities, impulses and emotions—are useful to us. Each holds a different piece of our experience and our character. Sometimes our parts have a distorted perspective or may use outdated or short-sighted strategies to protect and support us. Our critical part may berate us each time we make a mistake out of fear of failure—it may hope that if it shakes our confidence, we will avoid taking risks and will be safe from the threat of making a mistake. In the end, all of our parts are well-intentioned. Depending on the context, each serves an important purpose. Fear can be inconvenient when it shows up at our theater performance and makes it hard for us to remember our lines, but we're grateful to have it when it keeps us from doing something reckless like chasing a rolling ball into heavy traffic.

It is important that we allow space for all of the facets of ourselves. We may not want our more volatile or impulsive parts to be driving the bus, but there's no need to bind and gag them and throw them in the trunk. Instead, we can invite them to ride along as passengers, sharing their thoughts from the back seat while a more grounded, rational part of us drives.

OVER THE COURSE OF OUR life, our relationships with people will change. We form bonds, establish trusting connections, and then we must accept the twists and turns that life brings us—a friend moving across the country, the difficulty of scheduling time for socializing when work, parenting, or time with partners may demand our attention and energy.

Imagine there is a chessboard in front of you. Every piece on the board represents an individual relationship in your life. At times, we may move a piece closer to us—leaning into that relationship, prioritizing it, feeling a heightened sense of intimacy and connection. At other times, we may move that same piece a bit further away on the board, distancing ourselves—perhaps our friend has been unavailable to us lately, maybe we are focused more on a new relationship, maybe there has been a strain or tension that has made interactions difficult and we are needing space to get clarity.

Boundaries with the people we care about are fluid and we always have choice around where we position ourselves in relationships at any given time. This is useful to remember because it helps us to tolerate the inevitable changes, to be patient with gaps in connection, to remove the fear and judgment that may arise when we feel distance in our relationships. It also empowers us to lean in when we are missing someone or take a step back from a relationship when we need space.

There may be times we feel we need to cut off contact with someone in a more permanent way. Most of the time, however, changes in relationships are more subtle and may be temporary—all of the pieces on our chessboard of relationships in constant motion, a perpetual dance of intimacy and connection.

HAVE YOU EVER TRIED TO hold a chin-up for thirty seconds? For most of us, even if we are trying very hard, our arms will hold us for a while, then begin to tire and eventually we will involuntarily drop. Our body makes us let go before we strain our muscles to the point of injury.

Our nervous system works in a similar way. We have a limited capacity for holding an intense emotion. After a while, or if it gets too intense, it will automatically begin to drop off. If this didn't happen, we wouldn't be able to function very well as a species!

The next time you are sitting with a feeling that is difficult or uncomfortable, practice tuning in and really noticing everything you can about it—where do you feel it in your body, how intensely can you feel it? If you are anxious, focus your attention on trying to hold on to it. It's counterintuitive, but what you will find is that sooner or later, the feeling will drop off on its own. It may return quickly, but it is impossible to maintain it at its highest intensity.

We may hope that interrupting the feeling by avoiding situations or dampening our discomfort with drugs or alcohol may offer us some relief. In the long-run, disrupting our body's natural ability to cope with emotions reinforces our fear response and intensifies the discomfort we associate with those experiences. This may cause the waves of emotion to return more frequently and with greater intensity.

There is value in stretching our tolerance and increasing our capacity to ride the waves of our emotions. By doing so, they may carry us closer to the relief we deserve.

In Philip Pullman's classic novel *The Golden Compass*, twelve-year-old Lyra, the protagonist, is on a spiritual quest, armed only with a rare and mysterious compass called an alethiometer. Lyra is unaware of how the compass works, but is innately able to read it and must rely on it to guide her through situations where her own and others' lives are at stake.

Inside of each of us, we hold our own alethiometer or compass, fueled by our core selves, our inner values, and our most deeply held beliefs and desires. As we confront choices in our lives, we use this internal compass, or gut instinct, to guide us, not always fully understanding where it is leading us or how it is working.

The challenge for each of us is to remain in touch with the compass, begin to trust it, and be open to the messages it is offering about our needs and our aspirations. Like Lyra, ours is a quest of faith and may be wrought with doubt and uncertainty. Learning to let go and believe in our natural impulses toward self-fulfillment helps to ease our anxieties, simplify our journeys, and bring us a greater sense of peace.

CORMORANTS ARE SEABIRDS THAT ARE frequently seen holding their wings out wide in the sun. While many birds secrete enough oil onto their feathers to keep their wings dry, cormorants do not, so they engage in a wing-drying posture to speed up the process and allow themselves to more readily transition to flight after being in the water.

While their stillness and their openness in these moments may make them vulnerable, it is a requirement if they intend to take to the sky.

Like cormorants, we may also require moments of stillness and openness in order to fully experience our freedom, in order to achieve the gains we wish for ourselves, in order to thrive. In fact, it may be in these moments of vulnerability that we attain our greatest potential.

Our defenses instinctually kick up when we are afraid or feel threatened. Fear can be a skittish thing. When part of us is feeling afraid we may notice ourselves being sensitive, hypervigilant, behaving in ways that push people away or keep them at a distance. In order to relieve our sense of fear, we need to be compassionate with ourselves. We need to be patient and understanding. Approaching our fear with frustration, impatience, anger, or judgment will only make things worse.

Imagine you have just come across a stray dog huddled in the corner of a fenced in lot. It looks cold and scared, and you realize it has likely suffered some abuse and may even be injured. You try to approach it and it growls and bares its teeth. Rather than running up on it and trying to scoop it up in your arms or getting angry and shouting "No! Bad Dog!" at it, you realize it is just frightened and trying to protect itself. You stay where you are and speak reassuringly to it. You slowly move forward and set bowls of food and water a few feet away and then retreat even further back and sit down, waiting for the dog to assess the situation and decide whether or not it is feels safe enough to come forward.

There is a wisdom in approaching our own fears with patience, empathy, and gentleness. When we allow space for our fear to come out into the light, it may relax a little and may surprise us by becoming a valuable companion for us.

TAKE A PIECE OF PAPER in one hand and crumple it in your fist. Hold the paper ball very tightly just a few inches from your face. Keep it there for thirty seconds.

Now take the paper ball and rest it on the open palm of your hand with your arm extended in front of you. Keep it there for thirty seconds.

What did it feel like to crumple the ball? What did it feel like when you held it tightly in your fist, close to your face? What was it like to open your hand and hold the ball at a more relaxed distance? How did you feel about the paper in each of these positions?

All of us hold on to things. Sometimes we hold things very tightly. Sometimes our focus is very intense, and it is hard to see past what we are holding. Sometimes it hurts us or makes us tired.

When we shift perspective, open ourselves, relax our grip, we may still have the experience, or thought, or memory; that may not change. But our relationship to it, our experience of it, might.

Look at your crumpled ball of paper again. It's actually an amazing thing. You've taken one object and changed it dramatically. When scientists have studied the physics of paper and used an x-ray microtomography machine to take pictures of it, they discovered that even though crumpled paper is different depending on how it is created, the one pattern that appears in every crumpled ball of paper is that the flat parts of the paper ball always touch. They stack up, one flat edge against another. The more a ball of paper is compressed, the greater the layering. The greater the layering, the harder it is to further compress the ball. Although the volume of a paper ball is very low—it is ninety percent air—it seems to become stronger the more it is squeezed. The tighter we hold on, the stronger the thing we are holding becomes.

Consider leaving your paper ball on your desk for the rest of the day. What sorts of reminders might it offer you as you reflect on it?

You ARE STANDING ON THE edge of a high diving board for the first time. You are determined to leap from the board into the water, knowing that others have done this a million times before you. You know your friends and family are watching below, cheering you on, offering you encouragement, and bolstering your confidence. You have watched others dive many times before; you have read articles on diving form and have had others coach you in strategy, practicing your dives safely from the side of the pool. This, however, is the first time you are this high up. Your heart is pounding.

You can take a step away from the edge of the diving board to gather your thoughts. You can take some deep breaths and try to calm your fears. You can lie down flat on the diving board to feel more steady and secure. You can remind yourself of what you have learned and focus on the supportive voices beneath you.

Sooner or later, if you really want to do this, you're going to have to take a breath and step off that board.

Whenever we are taking a risk, doing something new, moving toward something we fear in order to master it, sooner or later we will need to act. Our thoughts are helpful to a point and then they may become distractions or obstacles. Get a read on your readiness for action, and even if there is fear present, remind yourself, "Don't think. Do." Close your eyes. Trust. And take the leap.

Dogs are generally thought of as attentive, loyal companions who are constantly aware of our presence and want to be with us every possible moment. Cats, on the other hand, are often considered aloof and inconsistent—much of the time, they seem to be avoidant or absent but will, on occasion, surprise us by jumping up onto our laps for petting, only to retreat again once their need has been met.

Grief can come to us in either form.

When we are sitting with grief that never seems to leave our side, that is ever present and relentlessly calling for our attention, we might call that "dog-tempered grief."

When our grief visits us on occasion, sometimes catching us unaware, stays with us for a short period, and then subsides, we might call that "cat-tempered grief."

Neither cats nor dogs are wrong or inherently bad in their approach. They are just different. Most pet owners know this and have come to appreciate the contact animals offer us in whatever form it comes.

Grief is very much like that. However it visits you—loyal and constant and dog-tempered or sporadic and brief and cat-tempered—see if you can remain available and open to what it's offering and do your best to treat it gently with appreciation and kindness.

DRAW A SMALL DOT ON a piece of paper. Now crumple it up and hold it tightly in your fist. Is the dot still visible?

Imagine that the dot represents clarity, insight, perspective. When we are constricted, we do not have access to our intuitive wisdom. It is always there, but we may miss it.

Our direct line to our inner guide—the one informed by our values, experiences, and instincts—is available to us when we find a way to open ourselves and to allow things to unfold organically before us.

IMAGINE PLACING A DROP OF red dye into a shot glass of water. The red color is quickly dispersed and is noticeable to us almost instantly.

Now imagine placing a drop of red dye into the ocean. The red is in there somewhere, but it is likely not noticeable to us and certainly doesn't change our perception of the seawater.

Emotions and experiences operate in similar ways. When we are suffering, it may be difficult for us to see anything but the pain. Our focus on what is hurting may color everything we see and make everything appear painful or threatening.

When our awareness is wide and full of an array of emotions, observations, and sensations, pain becomes just another small part of our experience. It draws less of our attention.

When you are suffering, instead of focusing your attention on getting rid of the source of your pain, consider expanding your perception and adding new elements of your awareness to the mix so the pain is diluted and becomes just one small piece of your experience.

IT'S NORMAL FOR US TO get tired. Working hard and striving to have the life we want isn't always easy.

Many of us want to think of ourselves as super-human and may resent the reality of having a finite amount of time and energy. When we are depleted, we may judge ourselves, become frustrated, or feel hopeless. It can be hard to accept our limitations and admit when we need assistance or relief.

Imagine you are driving in a car with friends. You're rolling along, bopping to music and enjoying the company of some of your favorite people. Suddenly the car shudders and then slowly rolls to a stop. You are out of gas. How might you respond?

Do you stomp around, kick the car, and decide to abandon it on the side of the road forever? Do you throw yourself across the hood of the car, sobbing, and plead with it to just keep going?

Maybe you feel disappointed or inconvenienced by the situation and then you sigh and accept you are going to need more gas if you're going to reach your destination. Maybe you roll up your sleeves, take a deep breath, and walk to the nearest exit where you fill a container with gas and walk it back to the car where your friends are waiting for you. Maybe you and your friends work together to roll the car along the side of the road to the nearest gas station. Maybe you and your friends wave down a passing driver to ask if they might help you get gas for the car. Maybe you remind yourself that, in the future, if you pay closer attention to the gas gauge, you might know when to fill up the tank before it gets too low.

It is silly to blame the car for running out of gas. Being out of gas is just a temporary condition. Try to remember that the next time your tank is empty.

NEUROSCIENCE IS LIKE THE INSTRUCTION manual for our brains. Knowing how our brains operate can help us understand our reactions and navigate choices in a more informed way.

Our mind is like a giant file drawer. When we experience something, we quickly consult our memory storage and pull out everything we can find—every story, association, past encounter—to help us make sense of what is happening. Based on what comes out of our file drawer, we have an emotional reaction to what we are experiencing and that determines our action.

Imagine you see a banana and think, "The last time I had a banana, I was nauseous." You may decide you want to avoid all bananas. But imagine if the last time you had a banana, you were sick with the flu. Perhaps "nausea" was accidentally misfiled in your brain under "banana" when it should have been filed under "flu." If you are able to walk back your judgments and return to a more neutral experience of the banana, you may find it to be a healthy, tasty treat!

Knowing that our brain, in the span of a nanosecond, may react to an object or a situation based on past experiences or learned associations that may have nothing to do with what we are encountering in the present moment can be very useful. It gives us the opportunity to walk our reactions back, to differentiate between what is happening in the reality of this present moment and what may be old stories or fears that we have been holding on to from our past. This allows us to have present-moment reactions that, even when unpleasant, are to scale with what is actually happening.

Knowing that most of the suffering we experience is a result of stored memories or judgments frees us to reconsider our encounters with the world with less reactivity and pain. Sometimes a banana is just a banana.

MOVEMENT AND PERSONAL PROGRESS IS a lesson in perspective. Just when it feels we are stuck and getting nowhere, we look back and realize how far we've come, how much has changed. The thing about formative moments—the kind we look back on and are grateful for—is that they are often painful, confusing, or frustrating while we are in the midst of them. Widening our perspective or allowing others to help reflect changes in us helps us get a realistic sense of where we are and the gains we have made.

Imagine yourself stepping onto an escalator. From your viewpoint, it may appear you are getting nowhere. You are still standing on the same step, holding on to the same rail. From a distance, however, your ascension is clear.

As social animals, we are constantly learning and changing. At times it may be hard to be patient with the process. Reminding ourselves of the distance we have covered can help inspire us to keep going.

THERE ARE NUMEROUS STORYLINES IN television, movies, and books that feature characters who, over the course of the narrative, become possessed by an evil force or inflicted with a terrible medical anomaly that results in uncharacteristic behaviors and a distorted physical appearance, sometimes making them almost unrecognizable. In *The Fly*, it was a science experiment gone terribly wrong. In *The Exorcist*, it was a demonic possession. In these stories, people who love the afflicted character are often horrified and repulsed by the exterior changes. By remembering the true nature of their loved one, they are able to maintain a connection and resist running away from what is outwardly unpleasant.

When we are in the grips of fear or are suffering, there are times our behaviors may be obnoxious, repulsive, ugly. We may use words that hurt; we may push people away or act toward others in a way that conflicts with our values. Often these behaviors serve as a defense to keep people from getting close enough to hurt us. When our fear or suffering is driving, it can be hard for people we care about to lean in close to us.

When you interact with someone whose behavior is problematic or annoying, see if you can relate to the vulnerable, fearful part of them that may lie underneath the off-putting exterior. Do what you need to do to protect yourself by keeping a distance or holding a boundary, if that is necessary for staying safe. Stretch yourself to see past the defensiveness, and remember what it feels like for you when you are in the grips of your emotions.

Compassion is what allows us to hold steady and maintain connection with what may otherwise drive us away. It is also what reminds us that our own ugly behavior may be a sign we are suffering. We can accept and offer kindness to ourselves and others while remaining vigilant and self-aware, which may allow the exterior to transform and the vulnerability to be revealed.

IMAGINE YOURSELF IN A ROOM, reclining on a comfortable sofa, reading a book. Suddenly, the door is flung open and a person comes in, engulfed in flames, flailing and running around. You want to help them, so you call them to you and reach out your arms. They run toward you, setting the sofa—and you—on fire.

Now imagine the same scene, but when the door is flung open and you see the person engulfed in flames, you take a step back to safety. You might shout out advice to them, "Stop, drop, and roll!" You might throw a blanket or a pitcher of water in their direction. Your first move, however, is to protect yourself and that choice allows you the opportunity to offer real relief or solutions without getting trapped yourself. When someone in our lives is struggling or is caught up in chaos or drama, before we jump into the fray with them, it may be in everyone's best interest that we pause. Start with making sure you are in a safe, solid place with perspective that will be useful and clear. Stepping back isn't abandoning or neglecting to help, it is the critical first step in helping. When our impulses tell us the most loving thing we can do is to sacrifice our own safety or security to help someone who is suffering, consider the possibility that putting ourselves in the line of fire may result in two casualties and may prevent us from having the opportunity to offer real, tangible support.

A BUDDHIST MONK ONCE OFFERED the following metaphor while leading a retreat: If you hold a flower in your left hand and you move it to your right hand, where is the flower? For most of us, the answer is simple. The flower is now in our right hand.

But that is only if we choose to accept it.

Interactions always involve two people offering one another their personal perspectives and emotional frameworks—an exchange of truths. We can pay attention and hold on to the parts of what a person is sharing that feel true to us. Some parts of what a person is sharing may not ring true for us. Perhaps in interactions with your father, he offers you his version of your relationship—that you are a son or daughter who does not appreciate him, that you do not value him enough, that he is not important to you. You may pick up this version of the story and carry it with you without even noticing it. You may find yourself feeling guilty or defensive, maybe even angry. You may respond to your father from this perspective and begin to resent him. You may avoid interactions with him as a result and find yourself pulling away.

Imagine what it might be like to pay attention and notice the "flower" he is offering you, to be able to observe it with compassion. You may see differences between the viewpoint he is offering and your own. You may see the ways you have made efforts to demonstrate your love for your father, to express your gratitude, to find closeness with him. You may be saddened that he is holding onto a perspective that hurts him. You may see the impact his narrative has on him and you may choose to reject it—to acknowledge he is holding it, but not take it on yourself. You can hope that by your choosing not to hold on to that story, your father may one day be able to let go of it as well.

It is easy to pick up other people's "flowers" when we are not mindful. Are you holding on to someone else's "truth" right now? Remember to own what's yours and what feels true to you. The rest you can simply notice and feel free to set down.

MOST OF US FIND THE idea of our own mortality unsettling or even frightening. Death, however, is a fact of life and something all of us as humans share. While thoughts about death may be experienced as distressing or morbid, confronting the reality of our limited time and energy can also offer us perspective on what matters most.

What would you most want to be remembered for after you die? What would you hope other people would say about you as they reflect on the impact of your life? What kind of legacy do you wish to leave behind?

Our passions and motivations are deeply personal. While one person may dream of starting a corporation and amassing huge financial profits, another may wish to create a piece of art that moves someone, or change the lives of family and friends for the better simply by loving them.

Whatever you find feels most important to you, remember this is what feeds your soul and will influence your choices. When we are less attuned to our own values, it is easy to get distracted by what we believe we *should* be doing or by other people's ideas about how we *ought* to be spending our time. Take time now to remind yourself of what matters most to you and come back to what you feel are the priorities most deserving of your attention and focus.

THESE DAYS, MANY OF US rely on some form of technology to guide us through our travels. Whether we're using an external GPS device, a smartphone, or an automated navigation system in our car, we are often steering ourselves with the assistance of some sort of tracking system. These tools can make transporting ourselves much more efficient and less stressful.

Outside of our vehicles, we are also utilizing a guidance system as we navigate life choices, relationships, and other human experiences. Our instincts, values, and core beliefs are constantly tracking each step we are taking and offer us feedback to help prevent disappointments, distractions, and losses. Not all of us choose to tune in to our internal GPS. Sometimes we may ignore or silence it, but it is always there and always aligned.

Think back to the last time you were using a mapping device to navigate a trip. If you missed a turn, ventured off-route, or got yourself turned around, did the device judge you, yell at you, or refuse to continue to navigate for you? Of course not. More likely it simply rerouted you, perhaps without you even noticing. These systems are built to assume variations and changes in our travels and adapt accordingly.

Now think back to the last time you made an important choice in your life. Did you question yourself? Did you worry that you might be making a mistake? Did you later judge yourself or feel regret for not taking a different path?

Every choice presents a new possibility and the loss of another possibility. Perhaps if we approached our decisions with more flexibility and compassion, we might reduce our distress, improve our outlook, and be more open to the twists and turns life has to offer us.

PICTURE YOURSELF FACING A BLANK wall in the middle of which is a single screw. You—provided with only a hammer—are asked to remove the screw from the wall. Could you do it?

Of course you could. You might leave a gaping hole of crumbling plaster where the screw pulled free from the wall, but you could get it out using only the hammer.

Now imagine you are given a screwdriver and asked to complete the same task. You might find it easier to do and that it results in less damage to the surrounding area.

At any moment in our lives, all we have to get us through are the tools in our toolbox at that time. Sometimes our coping mechanisms will be efficient and constructive. Other times, they may be messy, clumsy, worrisome, or harmful to our health or our relationships. It is important to view our efforts compassionately and to remember that our limitations are temporary. We benefit from having choices and a variety of options for how to cope. If provided with tools that are accessible and work well, we can minimize our suffering and make effective changes. Becoming healthier is a matter of expanding our toolbox rather than shaming ourselves for our attempts to survive with the limited tools we have.

For anyone who has ever ridden a horse, trust is an obvious component of the experience. A horse needs to sense a confidence in you—to trust you—in order to feel secure enough to let you mount and ride it. And you must feel a sense of trust in the 1,200-pound animal in front of you in order to climb up on it and ride. Experienced riders who have invested years in advanced learning, have practiced tirelessly, and have built a relationship with their horse may get to a point where the communication and trust between them and their horse is simply understood. These riders can run their horse through a course and know they and the horse are in sync. They can even let go of the reins for a moment and trust the horse is practiced and disciplined enough to know what to do. How invigorating it must be for both the horse and the rider to feel that free!

Some moments in our lives may require us to be vigilant and focused. They may require our full attention and awareness. We may find ourselves gathering the data, weighing options, and calculating potential risks. In these moments, we are learning.

There are other times when our learning is sufficient and we've reached a point of readiness. At those times, we may need to let go of the reins and ride, knowing we have done our due diligence and believing that we will end up where we need to be. In these moments, we are trusting.

How hard is it for you to let go of the reins and trust? What would it be like to feel freed up enough to relax your sense of control and just ride?

S OME TIME BETWEEN NINE AND fourteen months of age, most of us take our first steps. Our movements are tentative, sometimes clumsy, or inefficient. Our bodies are still new to us and we have not yet mastered the art of control. We use walls, furniture, and caregivers' hands to steady us while we find our footing and the courage to put our weight out in front of us.

We've all watched toddlers walking alongside their caregivers, holding tightly to a supportive hand, then rushing forward in the thrill of self-sufficiency. They often take several strides, then look back to ensure the safety of their caregiver is still within reach; they may even return quickly to make contact for a moment and then charge forward on their own again.

As we navigate changes throughout our life, we too may feel the exhilaration of our own agency. With enthusiasm alongside a healthy sense of nervousness, we step forward into uncertainty with a faith that we will be able to hold ourselves up and that even if we fall, someone is not far and will help us up again. It may be useful for us to remember those wobbly first steps and the wisdom of reassuring ourselves and keeping touchstones close at hand. Our sense of balance is not just about our own capacity, but about the faith that falling down is survivable and that someone will be there to help us rise again.

PICTURE YOURSELF STANDING ON A dock when you notice someone you love struggling in the water just six feet from where you are standing. They have clearly been caught in some kind of undertow and are fighting to keep from being pulled out to sea. With horror, you watch as they scramble to keep their head above water. While your initial impulse may be to jump in immediately and try to save them, you are aware that you too might be caught and may not only be powerless to help your loved one, but in danger of drowning yourself.

It is agonizing to watch people we care about suffering or in pain. We may be compelled by our desperate desire to help. It is wise, however, to consider that what a drowning person may benefit from most is a person with solid footing on stable ground who has a wider perspective and a greater capacity to offer the kinds of resources—perhaps a life preserver or strong rope—that could actual save them. Similarly, a loved one in emotional pain may benefit from us helping them access a support resource or a trained professional who may be better equipped to assist them.

Often, we feel guilty taking care of ourselves when we know others around us are suffering. We may feel selfish or neglectful. We may worry we are not doing enough, that we are abandoning someone who may need us. If everyone jumps into the current, no one is positioned to help ground anyone. Next time you are tempted to sacrifice your own needs in order to help someone else, consider resisting the impulse to dive into the chaos and instead solidify your own standing. It may, in fact, offer the greatest chance of survival for both of you.

ANXIETY IS A USEFUL EMOTION. As humans, we have evolved to generate an anxiety response when we perceive threats, so that we can respond quickly and avoid danger. In a crisis, we bypass the thinking, analyzing part of our brain and go right to reflexive action. When a lion is chasing us, taking time to assess, reflect on our fear, or strategize may result in us becoming dinner for a wild animal! Instead, our instincts take over, our breathing becomes shallow, our heart rate increases, our muscles tense—in an instant, we prepare our body to fight, freeze, or flee.

Day to day, most of us move about with relatively few life-threatening risks before us. It's unlikely any of us will encounter a ferocious lion on our way to work in the morning. Unfortunately, our hard-wiring hasn't been updated, so our survival response remains intact and easily triggered. Now, instead of preparing to run from an angry lion, we prepare to "run" from things that result in difficult emotions or that make us feel uncomfortable.

Our brain in survival mode doesn't differentiate between actual threats and perceived threats. These days, our fears may be less tangible. We may be frightened by thoughts, imagining potential losses. For most of us, our feelings are now the lion we are running from. Our body may still respond in primitive ways—bypassing our critical thinking, breathing shallowly, our heart racing, our muscles tense. We may feel like we are going to die even when we are in no imminent danger. Think about the last time you experienced this kind of stress response. In actuality, what was the biggest threat you were facing?

We may not be able to fully control our automatic responses to stressors. Mindfulness, however, allows us to notice we are having a reaction and gives us the option to slow down and check. Am I actually in danger? Even if this came to pass, could I survive it? Besides being uncomfortable or having to sit with a hard feeling, what am I actually running from?

Paying attention and remembering our brain is imperfect and may mistakenly sound an alarm when there is no real danger, empowers us to override automatic responses and make choices about how we respond. We can remind ourselves we are safe with our feelings and despite what it sometimes feels like, they really won't gobble us up.

THE PROCESS OF FINDING A compatible dating partner can be exciting as well as frustrating and discouraging at times. Imagine for a moment that we all have a perfectly calibrated machine inside of us into which we feed information about our values, preferences, and ideals. This machine serves to weed out potential partners who fail to meet certain key measures. Initial screenings may be broad—are they attractive, are they intelligent, are they employed? As individuals clear levels, the standards against which they are measured may become more specific and discerning—are they an initiator, are they comfortable talking about feelings, are they a good communicator?

Theoretically, with enough insight and experience, our internal screening tool should work to effectively identify whose characteristics match the type of partner for which we are ideally suited. The system, however, includes a major flaw in design—our ability to ignore or discount our internal instincts and best judgments.

Certain conditions—loneliness, low self-esteem, fear of rejection—may cause us to override our internal filters and overlook data that may be a sign of incompatibility. Sure, she's emotionally volatile, but most of the time she's pretty calm. Yeah, he's always canceling plans or not returning phone calls, but maybe this is just a busy time for him. While everyone has the capacity to change and to learn how to be a better partner to us, sometimes we will adjust our expectations or settle for a dynamic that is "good enough" rather than sitting with our loneliness or yearning.

Not only is it understandable for us to sometimes pursue relationships we instinctually know may not be sustainable, these relationships may be important opportunities for learning. Even short-lived or mismatched relationships may offer us a chance to more clearly identify our needs and practice asserting ourselves.

What may be useful is to notice when we've given someone a pass despite our better judgment. Be curious about why you chose to make an exception and try to be mindful of the data you are receiving, even when you feel resistant to it. By allowing yourself the chance to make less-than-perfect choices, you may hone your ability to read people and become more adept at identifying those who are like-valued and well-suited to be good partners.

ALL OF US ARE MADE up of different parts. We may have a part of us that is professional and confident that we present when we are at work or at a job interview. We may have a part of us that is like a baby, that sometimes wants to curl up into a ball and be taken care of. We may have a part of us that is an internal critic, our own bully voice that judges us when we make mistakes. In different situations, we may lead with different parts of ourselves. Sometimes the choice may be strategic—for instance, not letting our temper-tantrum voice respond to our boss. Other times, deciding which part of us gets to have a voice may be outside of our awareness.

It's kind of like having a microphone set up in a large auditorium. Depending on the conditions and context, different parts of us may want to step up to the microphone to express themselves. Our moderator part gets to decide who is invited to step up and have their voice be heard in any given moment. Being able to notice when parts of us have taken the stage and are speaking for us allows us to make more conscious choices about our voice. While all of our parts have a purpose and are useful in their own ways, some of our parts can speak in extremes, overwhelm people, or lead us away from what is in our best interest.

Let's say you're someone who is very shy and self-conscious and you are wanting to date. A coworker on whom you've had a crush approaches you and asks if you'd like to get coffee after work. Your judgmental part may get nervous that if this coworker really gets to know you, they may reject you. In an attempt to protect you, this part may tell you critical things about yourself causing you to doubt yourself, lowering your confidence and resulting in you turning down the invitation. Your fear part may sense the potential of you getting attached to your coworker and then possibly losing that connection in the future. That part may tell you that getting coffee is a terrible idea and will only lead to heartbreak. Your more grounded, confident part may be thrilled by the opportunity and may enthusiastically accept the invitation.

It's good for us to make time to listen with patience and compassion to all of our parts. Knowing our parts and recognizing what drives them allows us to decide which of our internal voices we want to invite to respond in different situations.

MOUNTAIN BIKING IS NOT A sport for the faint of heart. Trails can be steep and treacherous and require tremendous skill, balance, and focus. Like life, those who have the most success tend to take each turn or bump as it comes, keeping the long view and not getting distracted trying to anticipate every possible obstacle.

Avid mountain bikers know that when you've ridden the same trail repeatedly, the ground will form a natural groove into which the bike will be pulled. The more passes over the trail, the deeper the groove becomes and the harder it is to pull out and trace a new path.

All of us have established patterns or routines in our thinking and functioning. Any shift requires an awareness of the inevitable pull we may feel toward what is familiar and ingrained. It takes effort not to fall into the same old rut. Repeatedly pulling ourselves out of one track and onto a new path will form new grooves. The ride will gradually feel easier and more natural and will require less effort and focus. Of course, those ruts in the ground will always be there and occasionally we may find ourselves slipping back into our old way of doing things. This is not cause for worry. If we can notice we've slipped off the path, we can pick ourselves up out of one groove and into one that better serves us.

NYCTINASTY IS A TERM REFERRING to the natural, rhythmic process of a flower closing its petals in response to changes in light or temperature. On cooler evenings, flowering plants may pull their petals in, holding them tightly closed until the morning when the sun warms the earth and cues the flower to open itself again.

These times of closing and opening again are normal and adaptive, just as we all find ourselves at times needing to retreat or pull back. Our process, too, is driven by instinct, internal rhythms, or sensitivity to environmental cues. It is important for us to tune in and respect our impulses to turn inward, just as it is important to remember that in order to survive and to continue to bring beauty into the world, we must open ourselves once again and face into the sun.

INEVITABLY, AS WE MOVE THROUGH life, we encounter obstacles. Rather than seeing the challenges before us as insurmountable and giving up, we can slow down, assess what is blocking us, and identify the best strategy for getting around it. Obstacles can test how badly we want something and can motivate us to generate creative solutions for working things out.

If you were driving to work and saw an empty soda can on the road in front of you, how would you respond? Would you turn your car around and go back home? What if, instead of being a soda can, it was a cement wall? What if, despite appearing solid and ominous, the wall was actually made of crepe paper? Every obstacle presents us with a challenge—how big that challenge is and how much effort or creativity may be required to overcome it will vary.

Instead of feeling defeated or discouraged, the next time you find yourself facing a challenge, size it up. Get curious and creative and get an accurate read of what is standing between you and your goal. If you are determined enough, you can often find a way over, around, or right through whatever is blocking you.

IMAGINE STANDING AT THE EDGE of a beach, quietly watching as the waves roll in and then rhythmically retreat. There is a natural beauty to the movement—something most of us would describe as relaxing, perhaps comforting.

How often do you find yourself standing on a beach, panicking that the rolling wave that just left the shore will never return again? How likely is it that you would find yourself worrying that the tide would shift and disappear forever, leaving the land dry and lifeless?

Within our lives, there is constant movement and change—in our relationships, our level of productivity, our misfortune, and our joyful moments. Nothing is constant. What would it mean for us to have the same faith in ourselves that we have in the sea? To understand that, at times, the waves go out and at other times, the waves come in. How might we save ourselves from suffering unnecessarily and instead practice relying on the inevitability of these often unpredictable shifts?

The waves go out. The waves come in.

It feels wonderful when good and useful things flow our way. We need to remember the ebb times are a gift too. If we can avoid getting pulled away by our fear, we may find that the energy moving away from us is really just building itself up to return something amazing when it touches us again.

THINK OF YOUR MOST PRIZED possession, something that brings you joy and has special meaning for you. Now imagine you store that object in a closet, a closet that happens to be overflowing with a bunch of other junk you'd rather not sort through and organize at the moment. You push the other stuff out of the way, trying not to get overwhelmed by everything being in disarray, and push the closet door closed.

Soon, you are feeling a yearning for your prized possession, but then you remember that it's jammed in that closet that is overflowing with all of those other things. You don't feel up for dealing with that mess. So you leave your prized possession in the closet.

Another day passes and you're really longing for your prized possession. You're filled with dread at the idea of opening that door though—what if other things come tumbling out? You want those things to stay hidden away. You just want access to the thing that brings you joy.

You have a choice. You can decide to never open that door again. Yes, that would mean you would lose access to your prized possession forever and would have to accept not having it in your life, but you would also not have to deal with that mess lurking in there. Or you can open the door and accept that some unexpected things may tumble out. Maybe you'd have to put in a little work to get those stuffed back in the closet. Or maybe you would decide it's worth it to gradually take inventory of what's in there, install a few shelves, pack some items in boxes with the contents labeled so you'll know where everything is the next time you go searching in there.

Some emotions and memories feel valuable to us and bring us joy. Other emotions may be messier, more disorganized, and may overwhelm us. All of them are stored in the same place inside us—our heart. When we decide to close off to certain emotions, we may not realize we are also giving up access to other, more valuable emotions. Knowing what we've got stored in our heart and being willing to tackle the mess of it all allows us to have access to the full range of our experience so we don't miss out on the really good stuff.

Picture yourself standing in a bright, spacious kitchen. Behind you are shelves and shelves of every possible food you can imagine. You are surrounded by an endless supply of all of the sustenance you need. You, however, are facing away from it and may be unaware of what is available to you.

Now imagine that you are terribly hungry. The doorbell rings and you open the door to find a person standing there, holding a large box of pizza. The delivery person shouts, "Pizza delivery!" and as they offer the pizza to you they say, "That'll be $500."

Now, if you are truly without food and see no other options for obtaining food, grossly overpaying for a pizza would not be a foolish choice. In fact, it may be a wise decision. If, however, you were to simply turn around to more fully take in what was available to you, spending $500 on a pizza would seem unnecessary.

There are moments in our lives when we lose sight of the wealth of resources and opportunities to which we have access. In those moments, when we are viewing the world through a lens of deficit, we may mistakenly believe that whatever presents itself to us is our only choice, even if it is inadequate or costs us greatly. We may fear that if we reject what is before us, we are doomed to go without, that we will suffer and never have our needs met. We may approach job opportunities or potential dating partners or friendships from this desperate perspective. Choosing options that are insufficient or require us to sacrifice in unreasonable ways is not stupid. It is simply an indication that the other options may not be immediately visible or accessible to us in that moment.

Even if someone close to us tries to convince us there are better opportunities to come or tries to remind us that we are surrounded by all that we need, trusting and turning down the "pizza" requires a leap of faith. Sometimes in order to feed ourselves what we most need, we need to remind ourselves that what is available and what we deserve are not always immediately apparent to us.

S IT ACROSS FROM SOMEONE AND clasp your hands together with theirs. Have the other person press hard against you while you resist—pushing back against the pressure. Hold this position for ten to fifteen seconds. Now open your hands but keep your palms touching. As the other person moves their hands, follow their movements, tracing the shift of their hands away from you, closer to you, up and down. Do this for ten to fifteen seconds.

What did it feel like to resist when they were pushing against you? Where did you feel tension in your body? How did things feel between the two of you?

What changed when you opened your hands and resisted less? What was it like to move with the flow without fighting it or trying to redirect or change it? How did things feel between the two of you?

When we resist or fight against something, it creates a tension or stress for us that is not always necessary. Sometimes practicing acceptance and going with the flow can be useful for us. When we open up and have greater flexibility, we may learn something from following and observing what happens – what others do, where they take us. We may understand something new or learn something about ourselves in the process. It may change our relationship to the other person or help us think differently about the experience we are having. Sometimes, allowing something or someone to move us will show us something we might have missed while we were busy with our own intentions.

LIKE A PUPPY ON A leash, our mind can, at times, be a pesky companion. We may set out to complete a task only to find that our puppy mind is pulling us in some other direction. Our mind is always scanning the environment for something interesting on which to chew. Fears, worries, and regrets are some of the thoughts our minds find most compelling. We all know how easily our brains can pick up a thought and spend hours chewing on it, turning it over and over.

Just like a puppy, we need to remember that for most of us, our brains are untrained. They are used to running free, being driven by pure impulse. With practice we can learn to redirect our attention. First, we need to notice the pull. Then we can, with patience and compassion, gently redirect our attention in a more preferred direction.

For example: You're at work trying to get ready for a meeting. You can't seem to focus. You slow yourself down, take a breath, and realize your brain has clearly stumbled upon a really juicy fear.

Gently and with a bit of lightness and humor, you redirect. "No, no, no, curious brain. I know how compelling that fear of not measuring up is. We're getting ready for our presentation though. Here, make a quick list of the most important bullet points."

Your brain starts to make a list and then pulls again, reminding you of how embarrassing it would be if you made a mistake in front of everyone.

Again, you redirect. "We'll be fine, brain. You can set that fear down. Our colleagues are all really nice people who respect us. Even if we make a mistake, we'll be okay."

As many times as our brain pulls us, we can compassionately redirect. We don't need to yank the leash, swat at our brains, scold them, or drag them roughly. With consistent, gentle redirection, our brain—just like the puppy—will learn to yield and will be more responsive to refocusing. As we practice attention training and build our capacity to choose where we want our focus to be, our mindfulness muscle gets stronger and it gets easier and easier, freeing us up to enjoy our journey accompanied by our newly well-trained mind.

IMAGINE YOU ARE ASKED TO put out a fire in a burning building. You have no experience with putting out fires but are suited up and sent in with the gear you will need to extinguish the flames. You would probably be feeling a great deal of apprehension and may be overwhelmed by the task at hand. You may doubt your ability to complete the task successfully and may be frozen with fear.

Now imagine you are a seasoned firefighter who is asked to put out a fire in a burning building. You have put out many fires in the past and have a practiced skill set for navigating the task. You understand and are aware of the risks involved and know there is potential for failure or that harm may come to you, but you have a level of confidence in your ability to carry out your job, having done it repeatedly in the past.

Fear is always present when we are taking a risk. Particularly if the risk is new and uncharted or our skills for navigating the potential threats are untested. The more practiced we are at confronting and navigating the risk, the more confident we become. Do not mistake this for fearlessness, as having no fear when faced with a potential threat would be foolish. Fear is not an obstacle to our achieving our goals. It will be present. But it does not have to prevent us from having confidence in our ability to step into the fire and emerge whole. Every time we suit up and practice our skills, our confidence and ability to overcome our fear increases.

SOMETIMES THE ONLY WAY TO get out of something is to move further into it. Remember the bamboo finger trap toys you may have played with as a kid—woven bamboo tubes with two open ends. The idea was to stick a finger into each end of the tube and then try to get your fingers back out. The weave of the tube was designed to tighten as you pull outward, trapping your fingers in the tube. The lesson was that in order to release your fingers, you needed to push your fingers further into the tube, which would cause the openings to expand and loosen, allowing you to slip your fingers free.

Steven Hayes, the developer of Acceptance and Commitment Therapy (ACT) shares a similar metaphor using the idea of quicksand. He reminds us that most people, when they become stuck in quicksand, will panic and struggle, trying desperately to get free. In quicksand, however, these rapid movements will only make you sink deeper. Instead, the best way to get out of quicksand is to stop fighting and lay back, increasing your natural buoyancy by breathing deeply and putting as much of your body weight onto the surface, then use slow, deliberate movements to extricate yourself or roll yourself toward solid ground.

When we feel stuck, our impulse may be to panic or resist. That will often get us even more tangled up in whatever trap into which we may have fallen. Accepting and moving toward what we're entrenched in will often yield relief and allow us to identify a way out. The next time you feel stuck, try relaxing into it. It may be counterintuitive, but it's likely your fastest route to freedom.

It likely comes as no surprise that two of the most hunted animals in the world are deer and rabbits—two animals we often associate with words like timid, delicate, gentle, and soft. A couple of other animals that are among the most hunted are the shark and the tiger—animals that bring to mind words like fierce, fast, strong and menacing.

It is helpful to remind ourselves that regardless of our outward presentation, we all share vulnerabilities and can be victimized, overpowered, or frightened. It is also important to remember that deer and rabbits are skillful survivors who use their keen senses, balance, and speed to protect themselves and their offspring. Each one of us is equipped with tiger qualities and deer qualities. Some of these will make us vulnerable at times and some will help us stay swift-footed and a step ahead of potential threats or pitfalls. Connecting with the innate susceptibility we all share can help us identify common ground and increase our compassion for ourselves and each other.

THE TRIALS OF LIFE CAN take up a lot of our energy and headspace. Navigating changes, learning new skills, and confronting challenges can exhaust us and leave us weary.

When a skillful long-distance runner is preparing to run a marathon, they understand that it may take time to build the muscle, skill, and endurance necessary to sustain themselves. They may commit themselves to a structured training protocol, starting with shorter distances and building gradually toward longer runs or more difficult racing conditions. It would be unusual, and even foolish, for someone who has never run more than a mile to expect themselves to have the endurance necessary to spontaneously run 26.2 miles. It is likely they would never reach the finish line and may injure themselves in the process.

When working toward our goals, we may be impatient with our progress at times. We may hold ourselves to a standard that is unrealistic or that lacks compassion. There is wisdom in remembering our best chance for reaching our goal is to pace ourselves, to take breaks, to have people we trust cheering us on and to build our capacity incrementally. Hold the long view when it comes to motivating yourself and remember that slow and steady will often win the race.

MANY OF US EXERT ENERGY trying to keep our emotions in check. We may fear that if we are not hypervigilant, if we open the door to the feelings we are holding, they may flood in, take over, overwhelm us, spill out, and affect our choices, and we will never be able to contain them again.

While we can experience some emotions as powerful or overwhelming, all feelings are temporary.

It can be helpful to imagine a powerful emotion as a carbonated soda bottle. There may be tremendous pressure built up inside. When we first turn the cap and open it to the air, there may be an initial flood that may be messy and hard to control. We need not be afraid that it will never stop, that it will go on and on forever. The pouring out will end—either when the bottle is empty or when enough pressure is released that the remaining contents can be held within the container in a more stable way.

There is a benefit to periodically opening the valve on our feelings and relieving some of the pressure—allowing ourselves to cry when we need to, noticing when emotions arise during a yoga class, taking time to tune in to our emotional state. We don't have to feel everything all at once. We can learn how to open ourselves incrementally by refocusing or easing off when it feels like too much. And if we begin to get overwhelmed, we can remind ourselves that, like all of our experiences, this too will have an end and will change. Our greatest challenge is learning to bear the messy parts.

I MAGINE THAT EVERY ONE OF us has a pot of soup inside of us. Over the course of the day, we dole out ladlefuls of soup—certain activities or responsibilities cost us soup, certain relationships cost us soup. There are also things that put soup in our pot—maybe laughing with our close friends, hearing our favorite song, getting a good review in a workshop. There's an economy to our energy—soup goes in, soup goes out.

Imagine a pot of soup on the stove. If there is little to no soup in the pot and it's left on a hot burner, the pot will burn. That's the way heat works. It's science. It's not a reflection of failure or how committed you are or how much you care about things or how strong you are. We all have limits, and when we are depleted we will have less to give, less soup to dole out.

If we don't want our pot to burn, we have two options. We can turn down the heat—drop a class, extend a deadline, relieve some of the pressure we are feeling. Sometimes the heat is on whether we like it or not. In that case, our only option to prevent our pot from burning is to put more soup into it—whether by the ladleful or by one drop at a time. We can talk with a friend, go for a walk around the block, watch an episode of a show that makes us laugh, color a picture in a coloring book, bake cookies. Whatever puts soup in our pot.

Sometimes, when we are busy or stressed, we may feel we can't afford the time to take care of ourselves. We can't take a break, sleep that extra hour, or sit down for a meal with friends. The truth is, when we are under pressure to produce something important, we can't afford *not* to put soup in our pots. It's no good to leave an empty pot burning on the stove. When we take time to fill ourselves up, we have more to offer other people. We are more efficient and produce more interesting things. It is always worth it to take time to fill ourselves up and, when we notice others being depleted, to offer a bit of soup to them as well.

ALL OF US AT SOME point or another engage in behavior that has the potential for risk or negative consequence. We may eat the extra serving of ice cream, knowing it has a lot of excess sugar and empty calories in it. We may skip exercising and opt for watching television, knowing exercise would be better for our health. We may hurry across the street, knowing it would have been safer to walk to the crosswalk and wait for the light to change.

Risk is a personal calculation each of us make. We combine scientific data we acquire about potential risks, our perception of the likelihood of the bad outcome happening to us and the positive things we gain by engaging in the behavior and offset that with our level of motivation and confidence in our ability to make a different choice.

Take speeding as an example. Think about the speed at which you are comfortable driving while on the highway. Do you typically drive at the posted speed limit? Are you comfortable driving five miles over the speed limit? What about twenty-five miles over? Forty miles over?

Context matters as well. Imagine it is Sunday afternoon and you and your best friend are heading out to look at foliage. Now imagine it is Monday morning and you are late for a meeting at work. At what speed are you likely to travel in each of these scenarios? What factors do you consider when deciding the level of risk with which you are comfortable?

Behavior change is hard. When reflecting on your own risky behavior or when making judgments about someone else's behavior, remind yourself that behavior change is a process. Regardless of whether the decision is to smoke a cigarette or quit, to speed or drive within the limit, to go to the gym or not, have compassion and remember that all of us are doing the best we can in any moment.

IMAGINE FOR A MOMENT THAT you are wearing a pair of eyeglasses and in the corner of one of the lenses is a tiny spider. It is likely you would be distracted, perhaps even frightened by the spider and might try desperately to swipe it away.

Now imagine that upon removing and examining the glasses, you realize the "spider" was actually only a fleck of dirt. When you put the glasses back on, even with the spot there, you are more likely to ignore it, direct your attention elsewhere, and disregard its presence.

Our thoughts and emotions, especially when compelling or disturbing, are like those "spiders." Noticing them may be helpful, even more so when we have a sense of where they came from, but we have a choice as to whether or not to direct our energy toward them or to merit them worthy of our fear. Many of the fleeting thoughts and images that cross the screen of our minds are noise. They are temporary and baseless. By increasing our awareness of this, we can more easily direct our attention toward matters of greater importance and can avoid overreacting to threats that turn out to be figments of our overactive brains.

WHETHER INTENTIONAL OR NOT, WE can be deeply impacted by other people's choices or failings. Accepting this and coming to peace with the past is not about placing blame or directing anger; it is about seeing clearly and honestly the reality of our conditions and taking stock, in a compassionate way, of how those experiences may have changed or harmed us.

Imagine you invite me to have tea at your home and after twenty minutes, I jump up, spill my tea on your carpet, and say, "Oh no! I forgot I have somewhere I was supposed to be and now I'm late! I'm so sorry but I have to leave right away!"

Spilling the tea may not have been intentional. What happened may be understandable—it was an honest mistake. Still, regardless of my intention or how sorry I am, you were affected by my actions. You still have to clean up my tea.

When someone else's actions or decisions impact you negatively, try to hold compassionate understanding of their actions, knowing we all make mistakes under difficult circumstances. Remember to also acknowledge the impact on you—allow yourself to grieve your losses, to realize your sacrifices and to have empathy for anyone who is left to clean up someone else's mess.

I N THE MOVIE, *POLTERGEIST*, A mother of a child taken by an evil spirit is sent into a portal to recover her daughter. To prevent her from vanishing into the void herself, she is tethered with a rope around her waist before stepping through; this way, should she lose her bearings or be faced with a threat, those on the outside can pull her back to safety.

Taking risks, allowing ourselves to be vulnerable, opening up to something we fear may overwhelm us, can feel like stepping into that void. Knowing that we have connections that ground us, supports in place, people who will be on hand to pull us back and remind us of what is solid and safe can help us find the courage to lean into what frightens us.

What are your tethers? What relationships in your life tie you to the steadiness of your values? What pieces of art or writing, what words or sensations, bring you back when you feel yourself teetering on an edge? Find new ways to connect yourself so you can feel freed up to move in whatever direction your heart takes you and know that you will be okay and can always return to the space within you that is solid and comforting.

MOST OF US ARE FAMILIAR with the story of the three little pigs and their attempts to outwit the big bad wolf.

Imagine for a moment that it is the first time you are hearing the story and the telling of it goes something like this, "Once upon a time, there was a pig who built a house out of straw. The big bad wolf came along, blew it down, and ate the pig. The end." What would you see as the moral of the story? That we are all helpless and vulnerable?

Then imagine the story continued. "A second pig built a house out of sticks. The big bad wolf came along, blew it down, and ate the pig. The end." Now what would you see as the moral of the story? That any efforts we make to prevent something bad from happening are pointless because we are all doomed to a terrible fate?

When the story continues though and the third pig builds a house out of bricks, eludes the big bad wolf, and even manages to avenge the earlier pigs, the meaning of the story changes. Suddenly, the events come together as a story of hope and perseverance.

The challenge for all of us is to recognize that our stories aren't over yet. We need to resist the impulse to end our experiences with a period rather than a comma. Being patient with our journeys and hanging in to see what the next pages hold for us can change everything, including our perspective, in radical ways.

TREES ARE AN EXAMPLE OF nature's masterful engineering. Trees such as oak or pine that may grow in stable, temperate climates tend to have wide, ringed trunks and deep roots. Trees such as palm or birch that may be exposed to more severe weather conditions, such as storms or hurricanes, have far-reaching root systems and layered, flexible trunks. All trees have wisdom to offer us about surviving turbulent times.

Imagine that you are a large oak tree. You are solid and steady. Your thick roots reach deep into the earth. A storm may blow around you, shaking your branches, scattering debris, but you are solid and steady. You hold fast, unmoving, able to observe the storm without being pulled up into it.

Imagine that you are a palm tree. You are strong and flexible. Your wide network of roots stretches far beneath the earth, holding you in place. A hurricane may blow around you, shaking your branches, scattering debris, but you bend with it and are solid and steady. You may feel the impact of the storm on your branches but you resist being pulled up into it.

When our conditions are chaotic, tumultuous, or overwhelming, we can choose to be like a tree—solid, steady, and flexible. We can be present with whatever crashes over us and can bear witness to other people's storms, all while holding firm in a grounded, centered place.

I N MOVIES, DIRECTORS OFTEN COMBINE flashes of brief scenes in quick succession to indicate the passage of time. In *Rocky*, a movie about a boxer training for the fight of his career, we see a flash of Rocky tiring from a run, hitting a speed-bag, doing pushups and sit-ups, and finally victoriously running the 72 steps leading to the Philadelphia Museum of Art. We get a sense of what, in reality, must have been at least a month of physical training in under three minutes of filming. Video montages like this one are often set to evocative music meant to tug at our emotions and inspire us.

When we are in the midst of a transition or are working hard at making a change, sometimes it can feel like we are stuck and getting nowhere. We may have hard days, experience setbacks, or feel overwhelmed or discouraged. The next time you find yourself in one of these moments, imagine it as a flash in your video montage. Picture yourself accomplishing your goal and putting together all of the steps or individual moments that led up to your success. Now add your own theme song. Remember that where you are in this moment is just a snapshot of the journey you are on. Widen your lens and remember that even though it's so hard now, you're getting strong and will make it to the top to do your victory dance.

IMAGINE YOU ARE STANDING AT the edge of a large pool of water. Are you more likely to get in by wading into the shallow water, edging forward gradually while you acclimate to the water? Or is it more probable that you would dive right into the deep end with little hesitation?

There is more than one way to get into water.

Now think about a change you are wanting to make or a challenge you are facing. The uncertainty of the future is before you. Your goal is to get yourself into it—whether you gather your spirit and jump enthusiastically into the depths of it or cautiously dip your toe and step tentatively in where you feel safest.

A diver sometimes belly flops or ends up with water in their mouth and nose. It's okay if you jump and things don't go entirely as you planned. A wader takes their time and may miss the exhilaration of a sudden or impulsive plunge. It's okay if your path is slower and steadier. Lift the self-judgments you may have about your process and look around. Our future is vast and full of opportunities. Every moment takes us to a new edge. Remember the life you want for yourself, then look around. Are you in it? It doesn't matter how you got here. It won't matter how you get in next time. The important thing is to keep swimming.

HAVE YOU EVER TRIED TO carry a full bowl of water while walking? For most of us, despite our attempts at steadying our footfalls and maintaining our balance, some of the water inevitably sloshes over the edge of the dish and onto the floor. With each step, we may lose a little more of the water, until we are finally able to set the dish on a stable surface, or when the ratio of the water in the bowl and the space along the edge reach a balance point that provides enough internal space to contain the liquid despite jostling or tipping.

Now think back to a time you felt overwhelmed by your own emotions. A time when, despite your best efforts, you found your feelings spilling out. Perhaps you found yourself crying unexpectedly at work or experiencing an overwhelming sense of loss while driving to the grocery store.

It benefits us most to tend to our emotions as they arise, therefore preventing our feelings from backing up and overwhelming us. When we are filled up with emotions, it is natural for our capacity to hold things inside to be limited. The fullness and pressure of stifling what comes up can result in our expression of emotions feeling out of control. Allowing for some incremental release or "spillover" at times like this can reduce the volume of what we are holding and help us re-establish our equilibrium. As this happens, we may continue to be aware of our emotions sloshing around inside of us, but may now find ourselves able to more easily hold what remains.

THE AVERAGE NICOTINE CRAVING LASTS about three minutes, after which a smoker's compulsion to smoke recedes.

Every feeling we have can be imagined as a wave. We experience feelings as a growing level of intensity, a peak, and a dropping off. No emotion or feeling is constant. At times, we may feel we've been "anxious all day." If our nervous system was built to hold a feeling indefinitely, humans would die out as a species! It is more likely that over the course of a day we were hit with repeated waves of anxiety or that we experienced a particularly intense wave that wore us out. All feelings do eventually pass.

Understanding that feelings are impermanent and change in their intensity and duration can be empowering. Tolerating anxiety for a full day versus tolerating a wave of anxiety that lasts three minutes are very different things. Using the image of a wave to monitor our emotional experiences may help us track changes and remind ourselves that relief is often just around the corner if we can just hang in a little longer.

The next time you have an intense emotional experience—when you feel afraid, anxious, or terribly sad—try scaling the intensity of that feeling from one to ten, with one being only minimally uncomfortable and ten being the most difficult to bear. Wait five minutes and check in with yourself again. Now how would you rate the feeling? See if, over time, you can map out the waves of your emotions. You may even be able to begin to predict what triggers certain waves, the level of intensity at which they peak, and how long it takes to experience some relief.

BOUNDARIES ARE FLEXIBLE TOOLS WE use to adjust how much of something we let in and how much we want to block and keep out.

Picture a window in your house. The window can be shut tightly, curtains closed, no air or light getting in. The window can be thrown open wide, no barriers, letting lots of sun and fresh air in along with occasional mosquitos, flies, or blowing leaves. The window can be opened part way, screened and partially shaded, letting in some light and air but keeping out unwanted critters.

Remember you have choices and can adjust your boundaries as you need to. Perhaps interactions with your brother have been difficult lately. The last time the two of you spoke, he said something hurtful. It is reasonable you may want to protect yourself and may raise some of your defenses. If you cut off all contact, you may miss out on the nice aspects of your relationship with your brother—the ways he makes you laugh or helps you problem-solve when you're feeling stuck. You may decide to reach out to him even though a part of you feels a bit tentative and guarded.

You have more options than being wide open and vulnerable all of the time or being totally closed off and unavailable. You can open yourself a bit, see what comes through and make whatever adjustments you might need. Closed windows can stifle us. Having the option to open in small ways breaks our isolation, creates space for movement and allows the relief of connection to flow through us.

# AFTERWORD

THE PERSPECTIVE AND PRACTICES CAPTURED in this collection of metaphors reflects a set of values which are critical during this difficult period in our history. Being fully engaged, present and aware is more important than ever, but can tire us out and lead to fatigue and a need to recharge.

I believe, now more than ever, in the power of empathy. Flipping through these pages, it is my hope that the acceptance and compassion that underlie these words will have an impact. The practices are hard and tiring. The work is ongoing. Our hope is what will steady us and keep us moving forward.

# ACKNOWLEDGMENTS

I WOULD FIRST LIKE TO THANK the hundreds of clients with whom I have worked over the years. This book would never have come into existence without the inspiration I derive from our work together.

I offer much appreciation to Darla Bruno for help with editing and for cheering me on.

Lots of gratitude to Jen, Glendon and the rest of the team at MindStir.

Thank you to my sister, Christine Brandel, and to Michael Borum and Christopher Castellani for their enthusiasm, input and coaching throughout this process.

I would also like to acknowledge my teachers, in particular, Pema Chödrön. Your words and your wisdom have transformed me and made me a better therapist, a better parent, a better partner and a better person.

Thank you to all of my friends and family—for loving me and practicing alongside me.

Finally, thank you to Ryan, Antigone, Calder and Prudence. You are my roots and my reasons. You bring out the best in me and challenge me to stretch myself and the reach of my kindness and compassion. This book is a piece of that work.

JENN BRANDEL

# Photo Credits

Photo contributors include:

Karsten Bergmann, Christine Brandel, Jenn Brandel, Bruno, Isak Combrinck, Robert Daly, Guillaume de Germain, Alfred Derks, Mikele Designer, Jaroslav Devia, Danielle Dolson, Romina Farías, Victor Freitas, Alexandra Gorn, Eberhard Gross-Gasteiger, Guenter, Martin Jernberg, Maksym Kaharlytskyi, Kati "Tante Tati," SV Klimkin, Ylanite Koppens, Andrea Leopardi, Irina Logra, Gisela Merkuur, Liana Mikah, Carlo Navarro, Benjamin Nelan, Denys Nevozhai, Vidar Nordli-Mathisen, Mayron Oliveira, Maria Orlova, Theeradech Sanin, Marie Sjödin, Rudy and Peter Skitterians, Markus Spiske, Daniel Tausis, John Thng

# REFERENCES

Arbib, Michael A. and Bonaiuto, James J. (2016) *From Neuron to Cognition via Computational Neuroscience.* Cambridge: MIT Press.

Bayne, Rowan and Thompson, Kate. (2000) "Counsellor response to clients metaphors: An evaluation and refinement of Strong's model, *Counselling Psychology Quarterly,* 13(1) pp37-49.

Card, Orson Scott. (1995) *Alvin Journeyman: The Tales of Alvin Maker.* New York: Tom Doherty Associates, LLC.

Chodron, Pema. *Online Retreat: Living Beautifully with Uncertainty and Change,* October 28-30, 2011, Shambhala

Chorost, Michael. (2014) "Your Brain on Metaphors: Neuroscientists Test the Theory That Your Body Shapes Your Ideas" *The Chronicle of Higher Education: The Chronicle Review.* September 1, 2014. https://www.chronicle.com/article/Your-Brain-on-Metaphors/148495?cid=cr

Holmes, Jeremy and Bateman, Anthony. (Eds.) (2002) *Integration in Psychotherapy: Models and Methods.* New York: Oxford University Press.

Lakoff, George and Johnson, Mark. (1980) *Metaphors We Live By.* Chicago: University of Chicago Press.

Pink, Daniel H. (2005) *A Whole New Mind: Moving From the Information Age to the Conceptual Age.* New York: Riverhead Books.

Sapolsky, Robert. (2010) "This is Your Brain on Metaphors" *The New York Times.* November 14, 2010. https://opinionator.blogs.nytimes.com/2010/11/14/this-is-your-brain-on-metaphors/

Witztum, Eliezer, Van Der Hart, Onno and Friedman, Barbara. (1988) "The Use of Metaphors in Psychotherapy" *Journal of Contemporary Psychotherapy.*

# RECOMMENDED READING LIST

## *FOR ALL OF US*

Brach, Tara. (2004) *Radical Acceptance: Embracing Your Life with the Heart of a Buddha*. New York: Bantam Dell.

Brown, Brené. (2010) *The Gifts of Who You Are: Let Go of Who You Think You're Supposed to Be and Embrace Who You Are*. Center City: Hazelden.

Chodron, Pema. (2002) *Comfortable With Uncertainty: 108 Teachings*. Boston: Shambhala Publications.

Chodron, Pema. (2001) *The Places That Scare You: A Guide To Fearlessness*. Boston: Shambhala Publications.

Chodron, Pema. (1996) *When Things Fall Apart: Heart Advice for Difficult Times*. Boston: Shambhala Publications.

Germer, Christopher K. (2009) *The Mindful Path to Self-compassion: Freeing Yourself from Destructive Thoughts and Emotions*. New York: Guilford Press.

Goldstein, Joseph. (2013) *Mindfulness: A Practical Guide to Awakening*. Boulder: Sounds True, Inc.

Gunaratana, Bhante H. (2002) *Mindfulness in Plain English*. Somerville: Wisdom Publications.

Hanh, Thich Nhat. (2001) *You Are Here: Discovering the Magic of the Present Moment*. Boston: Shambhala Publications.

Hanh, Thich Nhat. (2004) *Taming the Tiger Within: Meditations on Transforming Difficult Emotions*. New York: Riverhead Books.

Hanson, Rick. (2013) *Hardwiring Happiness: The New Brain Science of Contentment, Calm, and Confidence.* New York: Harmony Books.

Harris, Dan. (2014) *10% Happier: How I Tamed the Voice in My Head, Reduced Stress Without Losing My Edge, and Found Self-Help That Actually Works-A True Story.* New York: HarperCollins

Harris, Russ. and Hayes, Steven. (2008) *The Happiness Trap: How to Stop Struggling and Start Living: A Guide to ACT.* Boston: Trumpeter Books.

Kabat-Zinn, Jon. (1994) *Wherever You Go There You Are: Mindfulness Meditation in Everyday Life.* New York: Hachette Books.

Kornfield, Jack. (2017) *No Time Like the Present: Finding Freedom, Love, and Joy Right Where You Are.* New York: Simon and Schuster Inc.

Kozak, Arnie. (2009) *Wild Chickens and Petty Tyrants: 108 Metaphors for Mindfulness.* Somerville: Wisdom Publications.

Patel, Meera L. (2015) *Start Where You Are: A Journal for Self-Exploration.* New York: Random House.

Salzberg, Sharon. (2017) *Real Love: The Art of Mindful Connection.* New York: Flatiron Books.

Siegel, Daniel J. (2010) *Mindsight: The New Science of Personal Transformation.* New York: Bantam Books.

Siegel, Ronald D. (2010) *The Mindfulness Solution: Everyday Practices for Everyday Problems.* New York: Guilford Press.

Tolle, Eckhart. (2004) *The Power of Now: A Guide to Spiritual Enlightenment.* Vancouver: Namaste Publishing.

Williams, Mark and Penman, Danny. (2012) *Mindfulness: An Eight-Week Plan for Finding Peace in a Frantic World.* New York: Rodale Inc.

Altman, Donald. (2014) *The Mindfulness Toolbox: 50 Practical Tips, Tools and Handouts for Anxiety, Depression, Stress & Pain.* Eau Claire: PESI Publishing and Media.

Burdick, Debra. (2013) *Mindfulness Skills Workbook for Clinicians and Clients: 111 Tools, Techniques, Activities & Worksheets.* Eau Claire: PESI Publishing and Media.

Burns, George W. (2001) *101 Healing Stories: Using Metaphors in Therapy.* New York: John Wiley & Sons.

Epstein, Mark. (1995) *Thoughts Without a Thinker: Psychotherapy from a Buddhist Perspective.* Cambridge: Basic Books.

Kopp, Richard R. (1995) *Metaphor Therapy: Using Client-Generated Metaphors in Psychotherapy.* New York: Brunner/Mazel, Inc.

Stoddard, Jill A. and Afari, Niloofar. (2014) *The Big Book of ACT Metaphors: A Practitioner's Guide to Experiential Exercises & Metaphors in Acceptance & Commitment Therapy.* Oakland: New Harbinger Publications.

# Index of Metaphors

Jenn Brandel